Introdu

C000178946

Travellers and tourists speeding along the A   ng a route that reaches back to Roman times but which despite that is actually a late developer among North Cumbria's roads. Now a very busy trunk road linking west Cumbria to the M6 and beyond, it is a product of a period of road building known as the 'turnpike mania' which swept the country in the eighteenth century. The Cockermouth, Keswick and Penrith Turnpike Trust was established in 1792.

Most of the motorists or motorcyclists that use the road probably pass the milestones that still exist along its length without even being aware they are there. This is not surprising, as compared to the road they seem insignificant. But the milestones between Keswick and Penrith weigh over 200 kilograms each and this does not include the cast iron plaques which weigh an additional 8 kilograms - hardly insignificant, particularly when account is taken of the skills and hours it took to fashion and erect them some 200 years ago. But there is something much more important than the physical aspects of the milestones. They are valuable artefacts, part of Cumbria's heritage, which should be cherished. Sadly they are so often neglected. Indeed, so neglected that they are vanishing at an alarming rate. And with their disappearance future generations will lose the evidence of how our roads have been developed and with it a piece of history is likely to be lost forever.

Milestones were an integral part of Turnpike Roads. Perhaps because Cumbria has such a wonderful landscape, which has been so fiercely protected by individuals and organisations opposed to the development of its roads, it still has an abundance of them throughout the County. There are over 300 still remaining. That is the good news. The bad news, as already stated above , is that many are being lost through damage and neglect despite the fact that many of them are listed monuments. Legally the Highways Authority own the milestones and has a duty to maintain them, but it is a duty that has been overlooked.

Over the past five years or so a few interested individuals, mostly members of 'The Milestone Society', have been surveying the milestones in Cumbria and forwarding detailed information of them to be entered into a national database set up by the Society in collaboration with English Heritage. In addition the members have been endeavouring to raise public awareness of the need to cherish these important and interesting roadside features. In 2006 members of the The

Milestone Society in Cumbria in partnership with the Keswick History Society embarked on a project to restore the milestones along the old Keswick to Penrith Turnpike Road. An important element of the project was to use the undertaking to provide educational materials which could draw attention to the need to protect the milestones and all the other ones in the County.

This route was chosen because it graphically demonstrated what has, and is, happening to these roadside features and because it had the potential to show how, with careful restoration and relatively moderate resources, they can enhance the Cumbrian Landscape. A successful grant application was made to the 'Local Heritage Initiative' (now the Lottery Heritage Fund) with the help of small pump priming grants from The Milestone Society and The Friends of the Lake District. The aims of the project were fourfold: Restoration of seven milestones; a photographic record of the work; a small mobile exhibition for schools, village halls, etc; and a CD presentation aimed at the general public, especially young people. This booklet is another outcome of the project.

Colin Smith
Brow Bottom,
Bowscale.

The Hutton Moor Road

A brief history of the road between Keswick and Penrith

It is well documented that the Romans built a road from Old Penrith (near where Plumpton is today) across the river Petteril through Lowstreet, Kelbarrow, Little Blencow, Greystoke, Whitbarrow to their Troutbeck Camps.

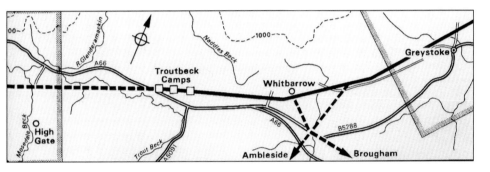

Much of the route is fairly clear both on maps and on the ground according to B.P Hindle[1]. It is conjectured that they also built a road through to Keswick but there appears no evidence to confirm this.

The Romans set up milestones, usually at every thousandth two-pace steps, and several are to be found today in the County, including one in Carlisle Museum. One can be seen today in a lay bye on the north side of the A66 to the east of Temple Sowerby - sadly the inscriptions have been eroded. Although chariots were used long before the Romans invaded, wheeled traffic in Cumbria was not common until the latter part of the 16th century. The principle method of transportation before then was by the sea with the west coast ports such as Whitehaven and Maryport being important centres of trade.

---

[1] Brian Paul Hindle, Roads and Trackways of the Lake District, Cicerone Press, 1998

4

In medieval times Cumbria's 'roads' were no more than tracks which received no organised maintenance. People either travelled on foot or on horses. In 1555 Parliament passed an act which laid the annual duty upon every parish to elect an unpaid 'Overseer of the Highways' to survey its roads, report on their condition, and to see that the necessary repairs were done under supervision by the parishioners. The Overseers were empowered to raise local rates and were responsible to the Justices of the Peace for their actions. Later, in 1691, minimum standards were introduced – for example those roads leading to market towns should be *'even, level and at least eight feet wide'*. It would appear this did not have very much effect on what roads there were in the Keswick to Penrith area.

What little transportation that took place away from the ports and rivers was usually done by pack horses. Trains of about 20 pack horses with hampers on their backs, managed by two or three men, were possibly the first haulage contractors. The pack horses were well suited to the difficult terrain of the Lakeland fells. Kendal was a major centre for pack horse operators with hundreds of horses engaged on such duties. By the 1770s it is believed that from Kendal alone some 254 pack-horses were entering and leaving the town every week. Those offering pack horse services prided themselves on their punctuality, promising delivery within an hour of a given estimate journey time. [2]

In the eighteenth century snuff became important. Tobacco imported at Whitehaven was transported along two 'snuff pack roads' identified by J D Marshall and M Davies-Shiel[3]. One of the routes was via Ennerdale, Floutern Tarn, Buttermere, Newlands, Keswick and on to Penrith. It is also likely that this route was also used for smuggling illicit spirits.

Thomas Harrison of Kendal took himself off to Glasgow to learn the trade of snuff making and

[2] Richard K Morriss, Roads –Archaeology and Architecture. Tempus. 2005
[3] J D Marshall & M.Davies-Shiel, Industrial Archaeology of the Lake Counties, Michael Moon, 1977

returned in 1792 with some 50 tons of machinery, all carried by pack horse, to set up a snuff mill at Mealbank on the river Kent.[4]

In 1835 an old gun powder mill at Eamont Bridge near Penrith became a snuff mill which continued with snuff production for almost a century. The mile had been owned by William Nevinson but it was later taken over by Samuel Gawith from Kendal, a company which manufacturers snuff to this day. Immediately after the First World War when cigarette smoking became popular, Samuel Gawith's was re-organised and the mill at Eamont Bridge closed.[5]

Penrith Museum has an engraved snuff box which has a lovely story relating to it. In 1820 John Dodd, who ran a saddler's shop in Penrith's Market Square was

driving his cart on the fells near Shap when mist began descending. After a while his dog 'Rolla' which had been running alongside the cart suddenly darted in front of the pony causing it to come to a halt. The dog ignored Dodd's calls to get out of the way and he was forced to get down from his driving seat. It was just as well, for he found himself, his cart and the pony standing by the edge of a steep drop and only seconds from disaster. Dodd decided to commemorate how his pet had saved his life in an unusual way. A cowrie shell was mounted in silver to make a snuff box and the lid was engraved to show a likeness of his pointer dog, with his own, and Rolla's name, and the year in which the dog had come to his rescue.[6]

With the growth of market towns those roads that did exist were found to be beyond the maintenance capabilities of Parish Councils. There was growing disquiet throughout the country about the poor state of the roads. The Government of the day decided that a new initiative was required. It determined new bodies were needed, Turnpike Trusts, to bring about improvements.

[4] The History of Samuel Gawith' www.samuelgawith.co.uk
[5] The History of Samuel Gawith.
[6] Sydney Chapman, Co-Curator, Penrith Museum

The Turnpike Age

The first such Act was passed in 1663 for sections of the Great North Road in Hertfordshire. It was not until the 1750s that Turnpikes really became numerous with over 400 trusts being established in less than 20 years - 'Turnpike Mania' as the period became known. Each Turnpike Trust was to be renewed every 21 years. Initially milestones were optional but the General Turnpike Act of 1767 made it compulsory for milestones to be erected.[7]

Between 1743 and 1828 some 26 Trusts were set up in Cumbria. The first Cumbrian Trust was enacted in 1739 at Whitehaven to serve the port that had been created in the 1680s by Sir John Lowther so that he could export his coals..

Legislation was passed whereby groups of people – typically landowners, traders, and farmers – could petition Parliament to pass individual Turnpike Acts which

allowed them to build new, or improve old, roads and charge those who wished to use them. Clauses were included in each Act setting out the conditions under which the appointed Trustees could operate - such as the number of Turnpikes permitted and the charges that could be levied. Turnpikes were usually gates or bars across the roads which were opened on payment of tolls to allow travellers to

---

[7] Act of Parliament 7 Geo III c.40, para XXX 1762. Cumbria County Record Office.

continue their journey. There were exemptions from paying tolls, for example for parishioners going to church on Sundays or to a funeral; farmers taking carts of manure to improve their fields; voters going to an election; cows being taken to or from a farmstead for milking; soldiers on the march; and mail coaches. [8] Notwithstanding these exemptions Turnpike Roads were not widely welcomed.

In 1762 Parliament passed:

> 'An Act for 'Widening, Repairing and Amending the Road from *Hesket*, by *Yewes Bridge*, to *Cockermouth*; and from thence, by *Lorton* over *Whinlatter*, to *Keswick* in the County of *Cumberland;* and from *Keswick* by *Dunmail Rays* and *Ambleside*, to *Kirby* in *Kendall*, in the County of *Westmorland;* and from *Plumbgarth's Cross*, near *Kirby* in *Kendall* aforesaid, to the Lake called *Windermere*, in the County of *Westmorland;* and from *Keswick* aforesaid, to the Town of *Penrith*, in the County of *Cumberland'*.[9]

It was one of the biggest Trusts to be set up totalling over 62 miles of roads.

The Act set out all manner of things including the qualifications necessary for potential Trustees, the places where turnpikes could be established and the tolls to be applied. A clause stipulating that "*stones or posts to be set up in or near the Sides of the said Roads, at a distance of one mile from one another, denoting the Distance of such stone or post from any other place'*.

Tolls for carts and carriages were based on the number of horses employed. For example "*For every Coach, Berlin, Landau, Chariot, Chaise, Chair, Calash, or Hearse, drawn by six horses or more horses, Mares, Mules, or Geldings, the Sum of One Shilling and Six Pence*".

---

[8] Carol Haines, Marking the miles – a history of English Milestones', Carol Haines. 2000
[9] Copy of the Act of 1762. *D/Law/9/44* , Cumbria County Record Office, Carlisle Office

In setting up the new Trust care was taken to ensure that the interests of all three towns along the route were properly represented. The Act enacted that the first meeting of the Trustees should be at the "*Sign of the Royal Oak in ,Keswick, aforesaid, on the Twenty-sixth Day of June One Thousand Seven Hundred and Sixty two, and shall be adjourn themselves from thence, to meet at Cockermouth aforesaid, at such Time and Place as shall be agreed and fixed upon at such meeting; and shall thence adjourn themselves, and meet at Penrith aforesaid,at such Time and Place as shall be agreed and fixed at such Meeting at Cockermouth aforesaid; and shall hold their Meetings, as often as Occasion may require, at Keswick, Cockermouth, and Penrith alternately and in Rotation*".

The original route from Cockermouth was over the Whinlatter Pass to Keswick and on to Penrith via the "Druid Stones" (Castlerigg Stone Circle), and then through Threlkeld, Penruddock, and Stainton. This is shown clearly on one of the earliest maps of Cumberland dated 1774, which was surveyed by Thomas Donald in 1770/1 (perhaps assisted by John Ainslie).[10] Each mile along the route is indicated by figures in the precise positions of the milestones shown on later maps. However there is no reference to them, despite the clause in the Act ordering them to be installed. The first map to refer to milestones on this route is

[10] Thomas Donald. Historic Map of Cumberland. 1774. Joseph Hodskinson
(Republished by Cumberland & Westmorland Antiquarian & Archaeological Society 2002)

dated 1823. This is in the one prepared for the Cockermouth, Keswick and Penrith Turnpike setting out proposed changes to the route.[11]

The first stage coach from London to the Lake District, drawn by six horses and known as The Flying

Machine, arrived in 1736 at the King's Arms in Kendal, and by 1775 the journey could be done in three days with a coach with steel springs. It was only the wealthy who could afford to travel in this way. Carriers wagons were introduced around 1753.[12] It appears that the influx of tourists and other travellers wishing to experience the tranquillity so eloquently described by literary figures such as Wordsworth was largely responsible for the increasing number of tourists [13]and with it grew the importance of the Keswick to Penrith route. This increase of traffic was not to everyone's pleasure. As early as 1791, a visitor travelling on foot between Penrith and Keswick commented that '*solitude and peace reign here undisturbed, except for the rattling tourist who excites envy and false ideas of happiness among the peaceful inhabitants*'.

James Clarke surveyed 'The Road to Keswick' in the 1780's, producing wonderfully detailed maps of Penrith and Keswick (amongst other places) and wrote in great detail about life, traditions, and history of those who lived along the route.[14]

---

[11] Cumbria County Record Office, Quarter Sessions CQRZ/2/9 1823 Keswick and Penrith
[12] William Rollison, Life and Traditions in the Lake District, Phoenix, 1997
[13] Paintings in the collection of Kendal Town Council booklet
[14] James Clarke, A Survey of the Lakes, 1787. Cumbria County Library Archives.

"The lands of this village (Stainton) are so remarkable for their fertility, that in the Spring of 1785, having occasion to go to London, I did not see any where,(either in Durham, Yorkshire, Lincolnshire, or Essex,) the corn in such forwardness as it was here"

Clarke goes on to write about many things associated with the area between Penrith and Keswick -

"Stainton,-Remarkable Family,-Old Sepulchral Remains,-Singular Antique,-Sketch of the history of the Knights Templars,-View of Greystoke Castle,-Account of the Noble Family of Howard,- Penruddick,-Motherby,-Roman Antiquities, Head of the River Petrel,-Stone-Carron,-Ancient Divisions,-Specium of the Language,- Mell Fell,Funeral Customs,-Strange Phaenomenon,-Terrible Inundation,-Saddleback Fell,-Threlkeld,-An Eccentric Clergy,-Druids Temple,- Castles,- River Greeta,-Remains of Buildings on the Banks of the River."

Clarke was not impressed with Penruddick *'a long,dirty, straggling village'* or Motherby *'a poor village'*. He considers it is worth mentioning

'Some singular customs in use at funerals in these environs. Notwithstanding some tenements in this dale are seven miles distant from Greystoke, they are all obliged to bury their dead there: all the relations of the deceased who reside within twenty miles, and all the neighbours, attend the funeral. A dinner is provided for them, and after dinner two pennyworth of wheaten bread, and a piece of cheese (by way of viaticum I suppose) is given to each person: the corpse is then laid upon a bier, and carried upon the shoulders of those who attend by turns, (a piece duty from which even the women are not exempted) till they arrive at a large stone at Greystoke town-head: Here they set the coffin down, and from hence it is carried to the church, (which is distance near a mile) by six persons, upon knapkins: during this latter part of the procession, the parish-clerk and people sing a psalm before the body, and walk, (be the weather as bad as it

will) with hats off. After the corpse is interred, the company
retire to the ale-house, where they are again refreshed with
bread and cheese, and ale."

Apart from the snuff pack road, which was no more than a pack horse track, little use seems to have been made of the route between Keswick and Penrith. Whitehaven was the main port through which tobacco was imported but most of it went either north through Carlisle and on to Glasgow, which was the major centre for snuff manufacture, or south through Keswick and down to Kendal. Even the main pack horse route from Glasgow to London went east of Penrith towards Appleby and Skipton. The first designated road in Cumbria since the ones the Romans built was a stretch from Kendal to Keighley, then the main route to London, was formed by an Act of Parliament in 1752.[15] The few people that lived between Keswick and Penrith rarely travelled any distance and those who came to exploit the area for its mineral wealth transported it to the coast for onward shipment via the west coast ports. The few tourists that did venture into the Lakes generally came from the south, via Kendal and Grasmere.

However as time went on there was local interest in improving the road and 54 individuals and groups took out mortgages to raise the £13,000 needed to fund this work. The Earl of Lonsdale was the biggest contributor.[16]

A further Act of Parliament was passed in 1824 permitting improvements and amendments to the route and then yet another one 32 years later states that – '

> *The Penrith and Cockermouth Road Act of 1856*
> 'The road commencing at the town of Keswick, passing through the townships or divisions of Keswick, Castlerigg, Burns, Wanthwaite, Saint John's, Threlkeld, Matterdale, Hutton Soil, Hutton John, Dacre, Stainton and Penrith, to the town of Penrith, shall be called "Hutton Moor End". The Act also authorised a new road to be 'made and formed, and afterwards maintained 'commencing by a junction with the Hutton Moor Road at or near the school at Castlegate, in the Parish of Penrith, and passing thence through the villages of*

[15] J W Dunderdale. Kendal Brown – The History of Kendal's Tobacco & Snuff Industry. Helm Press. 2003
[16] L A Williams. Road Transport in Cumbria in the Nineteenth Century. George Allen. 1975

*Greystoke and Motherby into the and as far as the Hutton
Moor Road at or near Becksis, in the township or district of
Hutton Soil, which shall be called the 'Greystoke Road'.*

This Act set out the tolls that might be
taken together, with certain conditions that
the Trustees and users must abide by. In
this act tolls were determined by the type of
vehicle being pulled or the number of
wheels it had. There was an
acknowledgement of the new power driven
vehicles that were to take to the roads
through the inclusion of the following
clause -

*"For every Carriage or Vehicle propelled or drawn by Steam
Machinery or other Power (except Animal or Manual Power),
One Shilling for each Wheel of such Carriage".*

Trustees of the Turnpike Trust were permitted to set a limited number of
Turnpikes or Toll houses, but restricted on the number of times per day tolls
could be taken for the same "horses, beasts, cattle, animals and carriages passing
through". Whilst the various maximum tolls trusts could levy were set out in the
Acts, Toll Houses were usually let by public auction by the Turnpike Trust
Trustees to the highest bidder, who won the right to live in the Toll House and
collect the tolls.[17]

There were a number of stables and
coaching inns along the route. The Sun
Inn at Moor End was for many years a
busy coaching inn but is now a private
house. Only the mounting steps remain
to give away its history. From 1790 to
1850 the innkeepers were a well known
couple called Hutchinson. It was said
that 'the old lady , who went on
crutches for the last part of her life, was

---

[17] Keswick Reminder. October 1881

a popular gossip, and no regular travellers when the coach stopped there failed to visit the chimney corner in the kitchen and have a crack with her'.[18] Stage Coaches from Lowther Hall to Keswick regularly made use of the Sun Inn.

There were numerous other Coaching Inns along the route such as The Horse and Farrier at Threlkeld, The George in Penrith, the Swan at Thornthwaite, and the Pheasant Inn, Bassenthwaite. Several more in Keswick are still open for business today.

Not everyone was happy about the development of these 'speedy' forms of travel – said to be "an incredible five or six miles per hour". Some learned doctors warned people from travelling by the wild and whirling vehicles as the rate at which they went would bring upon them "all manner of strange disorders, chief among which was apoplexy"[19] Local market holders and their customers were among others with whom the Turnpike roads were not popular.

When the Cockermouth-Penrith Trust was inaugurated in 1761, its Trustees were empowered to place a toll bar across the road at a point near Penrith Castle, at the junction leading from the villages of Blencow, Newbiggin, and Stainton. It was sited there to catch the market traders who came to Penrith. The Trust was supposed to maintain this road with money raised through

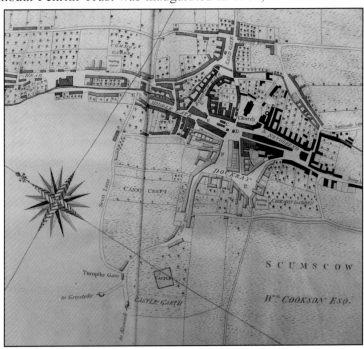

[18] Arthur G Bradley. Highways and Byways in the Lake District. McMillan. 1901
[19] Watson 1894

14

tolls but apparently it did little such work. Those regularly taking goods and produce to the market in Penrith found the tolls prohibitive, and people living in Penrith felt they paid too high a price for the produce because of the added cost put on suppliers to cover the cost of tolls. Both groups tried to find ways of conducting their business by avoiding toll bars by using other routes. Trustees of the Turnpike took steps to thwart such avoidances by applying for permission to install more toll bars. It became a serious dispute [20], but fortunately it did not involve violence.

Other parts of the country were not so lucky. There were incidents of toll houses and turnpike gates being destroyed, and even the murder of a turnpike gate keeper. So concerned was the government of the day that in 1822 it passed the General Turnpike Act which not only tidied up and repealed 16 previous acts but reintroduced the penalty for destroying a turnpike gate to *'Transportation to One of His Majesty's Plantations Abroad for Seven Years'* [21]

Between 1801 and 1831 the population of Penrith and Keswick increased by over sixty per cent. Their associated industries, together with the development of springs enabling wagons and carriages to move faster necessitated better road surfaces. Sections of the road were rebuilt in 1824 by one of the most famous civil engineers of the time, John Loudon McAdam. Along with Thomas Telford, he had become involved in Cumbrian projects. The Cockermouth-Penrith Trustees had in 1823 invited McAdam to recommend a competent surveyor to undertake road improvements. It was at this time that the route from Cockermouth to Keswick was changed to run alongside the southern shore of Bassenthwaite Lake, so avoiding the hard climb for carriages over the Whinlatter Pass. McAdam became personally responsible for the making of 10 miles of new road between Keswick and Penrith.

---

[20] L.A. Williams. Road Transport in Cumbria in the Nineteenth. George Allen. 1975
[21] Act of Parliament 7 Geo III c40. 1822. National Archives, Kew.

It would appear McAdam enjoyed Keswick as he lived in a house in the Town. However other towns in Cumbria also claim McAdam lived in their midst. Penrith Civic Society made representations around 1974 to the then Penrith Urban District Council to erect a blue plaque on the railings outside Cockell House in Drovers Lane which can still be seen. The inscription "John Macadam, General Surveyor of Roads, lived here c.1820 "In 1825 he surveyed the Penrith-Greta Bridge Road". This is not a plaque which was approved under the 'Blue Plaque' scheme run by English Heritage. The evidence for this claim seems obscure. It is believed McAdam rented houses in a number of towns in Cumbria towns whilst carrying out work nearby so perhaps he lived here.

In the 1840s passenger traffic on the Cockermouth to Penrith Turnpike Road increased considerably. In 1841 the Trust's toll revenues amounted to £1,456. 3s 1d; by 1849 they had risen to a total of £2,109 0s 10d.

The Lancaster to Carlisle Railway was opened in 1846 bringing rail traffic to Penrith and with it more tourists seeking the delights they had read about.

Railways continued to be built on in Cumberland and in the early 1860's the Penrith to Cockermouth railway line was constructed under an Act of Parliament dated the 1st August 1861. The Chairman of the Company cut the first sod in May the following year. The line opened to goods traffic in 1864 and to passengers traffic in 1865. The coming of the railways brought  increased prosperity to the Turnpike road owners, the number of tourists that they brought to enjoy the scenery they had read about increasingly. It was not uncommon for dozens of carriages to be waiting for the arrival of trains at Keswick and Penrith Stations.

By this time both Keswick and Penrith were each ringed with Tollgates. Any carriages or vehicles taking passengers on to scenic places such as Ullswater, Thirlmere, and Buttermere were obliged to pay tolls.

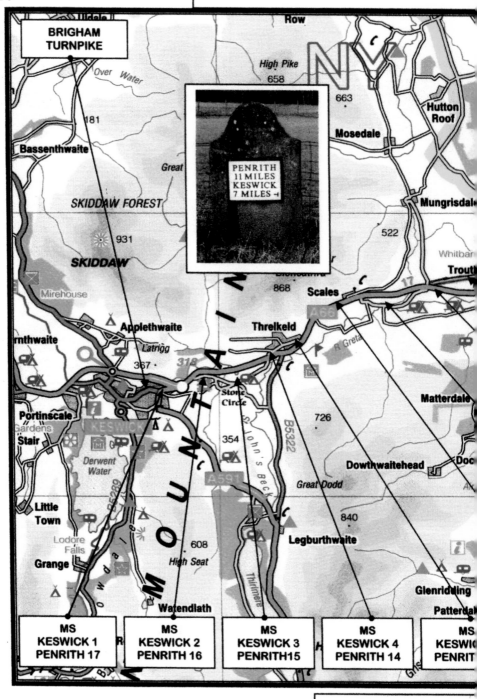

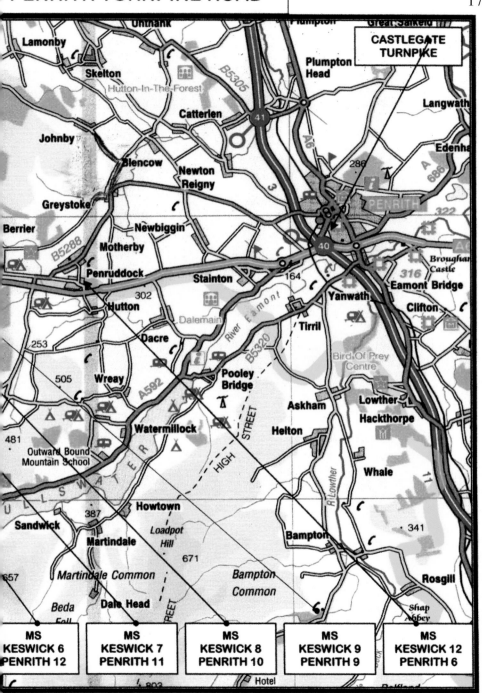

Mr Richard Rigg of the Windermere Hotel built the largest and most successful coaching business in the Lake District. On arrival of trains at Penrith and later Keswick, his Royal Mail coaches, pulled by three horses and driven by scarlet-coated , white-top-hatted drivers were a regular sight.[22] But to reach villages and hamlets the carriages, owned by Royal Mail but with Rigg's horses and drivers, were more modest. Hugh Lowther, the fifth earl of Lonsdale, or "Lordy" as he was affectionately called, had magnificent carriages in canary yellow with black wheels, and his coronet on the doors; immaculate chestnut horses were ridden by postillions in yellow jackets, white breeches and black caps and boots, and each carried a silver-mounted whip.[23]

Steam engines and horses did not always combine easily. In 1850 an accident involving the carriage belonging to the Rev. Henry Askew, Rector of Greystoke, is an example.[24] Coachman Thomas Brownrigg maintained that he was nearing the station taking 'three lasses from Patterdale to Penrith' when smoke "carelessly emitted from an engine shunting in the

sidings" caused his two horses to stampede, putting them in danger and damaging the carriage.

However after the early years of steam Turnpike revenues steadily declined. The introduction of smoother road surfaces caused problems for some coaching services in the area, particularly on steep gradients where the horses were unable to gain grip to pull or brake their heavy loads. In the long term it was neither surfaced roads nor the railways that posed the biggest threat to the dominance of

[22] William Rollinson. Life and Traditions in the Lake District, Phoenix,. 1997
[23] Irvine Hunt. Lakeland Yesterday - Volume 1, Smith Settle, 2002
[24] Coachman's sworn evidence. *D/HUD/4/3*. Cumbria Record Office, Carlisle 1850

horse transportation. It was the development of the combustion engine. The rapid expansion of motorised traffic caused much wear and tear with which the Turnpike system was unable to cope. The road system clearly needed a much greater initiative to meet the demands now being made on them. Like most of the other Turnpike Trusts, the Cockermouth to Penrith Trust was dissolved in 1883.[25] When County Councils were set up in 1888 the Cumberland and Westmorland County Councils took over responsibility for maintaining and developing roads in Cumbria. For nearly a century the route of the turnpike road stayed the same, apart from improved road surfacing, but traffic was to steadily increase.

In the 1970s , plans were drawn up for a new road to be built to service the industries in West Cumbria which would by-pass most of the Keswick to Penrith Turnpike Road. A very acrimonious campaign took place. Many opposed the building of such a major highway through the heart of the northern lakes, advocating that it if such a road had to be built it should be routed to the north of the Caldbeck Fells. The Countryside Commission proposed that the B5305, through Hutton in the Forest and Sebergham to just south of Wigton, and the A595 and be upgraded to form the new link with West Cumbria. The argument was lost, consequently many sections of the original Hutton Moor Road became by-passed. Today some parts of the old Turnpike Road are now either minor roads or have become footpaths and cycle ways.

The new road was made dual carriageway from Penrith to Penruddick although the westbound carriageway was little altered, using the existing road, with the eastbound carriageway being new and built to the standards of the day. The Threlkeld and Keswick by-passes built at this time.

When road numbers were first allocated in the 1920s the road between Penrith and Keswick was given the number A594. In order to encourage drivers to reach the Keswick area by way of the M6 and the upgraded A594 (instead of the A591 via Ambleside) the A594 was renumbered as the A66.

Seventeen milestones had been erected along the Hutton Moor Road all consisting of dome shaped Lakeland green stone. They had cast iron plaques bolted to them, giving distances to Penrith and Keswick painted in black letters on a white background. Although they may look insignificant each milestone weighed about 200 kilograms and the cast iron plaques over 7 kilograms each. Although several of them were discarded when the 1970s reconstruction took place. A number

[25] Cumberland Paquet, 12th February, 1850

remain, and one or two were saved by local people who currently have ownership of them.

Following restoration projects by The Milestone Society and the Keswick Historical Society ten original milestones, or parts of them, can still be seen today. They are to be found at Brigham, Keswick (NY280239); Storms Farm (NY294244); Shundraw Junction NY302240); The Riddings, Threlkeld (NY316249); Woodend, Threlkeld (NY326251); Scales (NY339267); Wallthwaite (NY354267); Lisco Farm (NY369272); Far Howe, Troutbeck (NY385272); and Penruddick (NY431275).

Turnpikes usually had Toll Houses alongside them and the Keswick to Penrith road was no exception. Only two remain today – one at Brigham at the east end of Keswick, set up under the 1762 Act .

The other, named Scales Gate, is situated on the north side of the A66 to the east of Threlkeld. This was an additional turnpike added in 1839.[26]

Whilst toll charges were set out in the relevant Act of Parliament the appointment of 'pike keepers' was made by the Trustees following public auctions as explained on page 12.

The person appointed won the right to live in the Toll House and collect tolls. The two that remain today are both now private houses. There are other houses still to be seen around Penrith and Keswick which were originally Toll Houses, serving different Turnpike roads from the towns. See appendix 2, page 28.

---

[26] Minutes of the Keswick Turnpike Trust, 27th April, 1839

The 2007 Keswick to Penrith Milestone Project

The Milestone Society was established in 2001. It now has over 300 members and an established county representatives' network *to 'identify, record, research, conserve, and interpret for public benefit the milestones and other waymarkers of the British Isles'.* Over the past few years members of The Milestone Society, together with a few individuals, have been surveying the milestones in Cumbria and collecting detailed information based on the template provided by the Society's national database. A national database has been set up in collaboration with English Heritage. From this work it is evident that Cumbria, compared to many other counties, has an extraordinary wealth of milestones. Probably this is partly due to the determination of so many people and organisations, such as the Friends of the Lake, to protect Cumbria's wonderful landscape by opposing road widening schemes.

Sadly though the surveys in Cumbria have revealed is that most of the milestones are shamefully neglected, even those which are listed by the Department of the Environment. Some milestones have been discarded when

road widening schemes have been undertaken. Milestones, particularly those made of sandstone, have been destroyed during grass verge cutting activities.

However a few have been looked after by individuals or local interest groups and show what attractive features they make – those in Cartmel are a good example. Some milestones have been 'rescued' and installed on private property. A few have been stolen.

In 2005 The Keswick Historical Society "adopted" one milestone at Wallthwaite near Threlkeld and obtained a grant to replace its missing cast iron plaque. In 2006 The Milestone Society in partnership with the Keswick History Society, embarked on an ambitious project. This was to restore all the milestones along the Keswick to Penrith Turnpike and to use the undertaking to provide educational and public awareness materials which could help draw attention to the need to protect all the other milestones in the County.

This route was chosen because it demonstrates what can happen to Cumbrian milestones when they are disregarded or neglected. All the milestones bar two are now on minor roads. It was felt that in renovating them they would be easily found and enjoyed by passers by'.

A grant application to the Local Heritage Initiative was successful and The Milestone Society and The Friends of the Lake District made contributions with 'pump priming' grants. The aims of the project were fourfold: Restoration of six milestones; a photographic record of the work; a small mobile exhibition for schools, village halls, etc; a CD presentation aimed at the general public, especially young people.

Surveys had located ten remaining milestones, or remains of them, along the Keswick to Penrith Turnpike. Five were intact although one of these had been re-sited on private premises; three had their cast iron plates missing but the stones themselves intact; two had been broken off and the tops and plates missing; and one stone was missing but the original plaque mounted on a private house. All of the

milestones had been discarded when the new road was built in the 1970s. Most of the sites needed groundwork to make the milestones visible and searches with metal detectors took place to try to find the missing cast iron plaques. It was evident the two milestones which were broken required protection to ensure further loss did not occur during grass and hedge cutting activities.

Two original plaques were found - one attached to Saddleback View, Threlkeld, the home of Tom Threlkeld & Mrs Hughes, and the other in the possession of Mr and Mrs Teasdale of Lisco Farm, Troutbeck. Happily both plaques were donated so they could be restored and mounted on new milestones erected close to the positions shown on the old turnpike maps.

The milestone at Woodend, Threlkeld was being crushed by the roots of a large sycamore tree and had a serious crack through its entire length. Tree surgery was needed.

The project determined to carry out all the necessary ground work, install four new milestones – two to protect the remains of the broken ones, and two to mount the original plaques referred to above.

A local company, Lakeland Slate Products, was commissioned to source stone similar to the originals and to prepare the new milestones in the traditional way. Suitable stone was found at the Quarry at Elterwater.

The new milestones have '2007' engraved on the back of them.

A specialist company, Sign Post Restoration Limited of Lanercost who had provided the cast iron plate for the earlier restoration of milestone (Penrith 11

Keswick 7 miles) was engaged to supply replicas of the five missing plates. This involved making wood patterns which were used to form sands moulds.

These were cast at a foundry in Hexham. The plaques were made in cast iron

much the same as the originals, perhaps the metal being of a purer quality than the originals. All the plaques, both original and old, were then painted. Wilson's Plant & Haulage Limited of Threlkeld installed the new milestones under the direction of Project volunteer managers, Colin Smith and Gordon Furness. The new milestone at the west end of Threlkeld village, to which the original plaque, donated by Tom Salkeld and Mrs Hughes of Threlkeld, was attached, had to be installed some 20 metres away from its original site that is is now in the middle of the widened road. The original plaques and the new ones were then fitted using stainless steel bolts with security fastenings.

The seven restored milestones

Brigham, Keswick (NY280238)

Storms Farm (NY294244)

Shrundraw Junction (NY304240)

West Threlkeld (NY315249)

Woodend, Threlkeld (NY326251)

Lisco Farm (NY369272)

Far Howe, Troutbeck (NY385272)

The project was completed in May 2007 and celebrated with the unveiling of the new Milestone at the west end of Threlkeld by Tom Salkeld & Mrs Hughes together with an exhibition of the project and the history of the Keswick to Penrith Turnpike Road in Threlkeld Parish Rooms. Among those who also attended the event were pupils of Threlkeld Church of England Primary School.

To Road Makers

AND

LABOURERS.

THE TRUSTEES

OF THE

PENRITH AND KESWICK

TURNPIKE ROADS,

Will receive Proposals in Writing, at the

New Crown Inn,

PENRITH,

On TUESDAY, 29th of NOVEMBER next,

AT 12 O'CLOCK AT NOON,

For repairing and keeping in repair for 12 Months, from the 1st day of January next, 1837, of part of the Turnpike Road leading from Penrith to Keswick.

28

Appendix 1
Designs of milestones on other Turnpike Roads which served Keswick and Penrith

A6 Penrith to Carlisle

A66 Penrith to Appleby

A6 Penrith to Shap

A686 Penrith to Alston

A591 Keswick to Windermere

B5291 Keswick to Cockermouth

Appendix 2
Ex Turnpike houses still to be seen in the Keswick and Penrith areas

**Toll House, Brackenrigg
(NY212326)**

**Toll Bar Cottage, Lonsties,
(NY278232)**

**Toll Bar Cottage, Brigham
(NY274238)**

**Toll Bar Cottage, Scales
(NY340268)**

**Lakeland View, Keswick
(NY261238)**

**Toll Bar Cottage, Eamont Bridge
(NY521289)**

Toll Bar Cottage, Brougham
(NY537292)

Toll Bar Cottage, New Hutton
(NY505338)

GENERAL STATEMENT OF THE INCOME AND EXPENDITURE

OF THE

KESWICK TURNPIKE TRUST,

IN THE COUNTY OF CUMBERLAND,

Between the 1st Day of JANUARY and the 31st Day of DECEMBER, 1834.

INCOME:

	£.	s.	d.
Balance in Treasurer's hands brought forward,	85	9	8¼
Ditto in Surveyor's,	7	4	11
Revenue received from Tolls,	1610	10	6
Parish Composition in lieu of Statute Duty,	0	0	0
Estimated Value of Statute Duty performed,	0	0	0
Revenue from Fines,	0	0	0
Ditto from Incidental Receipts	0	15	0
Amount of Money borrowed on the Security of the Tolls,	0	0	0
	1704	9	1¼

EXPENDITURE:

	£.	s.	d.
Manual Labour,	568	11	2
Team Labour and Carriage Materials,	95	19	6
Materials for Surface Repairs,	0	0	0
Land Purchased,	12	13	6
Damage done in obtaining Materials,	0	17	5
Tradesmen's Bills	57	4	5
Salaries:— Treasurer,	31	10	0
Clerk,	31	10	0
Surveyor,	99	12	0
Law Charges,	12	0	0
Interest of Debt,	640	5	2
Improvements,	0	0	0
Debts paid off,	0	0	0
Incidental Expenses,	21	5	2
Statute Duty performed, estimated value,	0	0	0
Paid Township of Greystoke, Johnby, &c.	30	0	0
Ditto ditto of Underskiddaw,	14	11	8
Balance in Surveyor's hands,			
Ditto in Treasurer's due the Trust,	83	9	6¾
	£1704	9	1¼

Debts.				Rate of Interest per cent.	Arrears of Income.			
	£.	s.	d.			£.	s.	d.
Bonded or Mortgage Debt,	13740	5	0		Arrears of Tolls for current year,	127	17	5
Floating Debt,	0	0	0	£4 10 0	Arrears of Parish Composition ditto,	0	0	0
Unpaid Interest,	233	16	4½		Arrears of any other Receipt ditto,	0	0	0
					Arrears of former years,	0	0	0
Total Debt, £13974 1 4½					Total Arrears, £127 17 5			

Insert the Name and Place of Abode of the Treasurer, Clerk, General, and Superintending Surveyor.

THOMAS HIXSON of Penrith, Cumberland, Treasurer.
RICHARD FISHER of Cockermouth, Cumberland, Clerk.
JOHN FLEMING of Greta Bank, near Keswick, Cumberland, Surveyor.

At the General Annual Meeting of the Trustees of the Keswick Road, holden at the New Crown Inn, in Penrith, on TUESDAY, the 24th Day of MARCH, 1835, this Account was audited and settled, and found correct.

E. W. HASELL, *Chairman.*

List of drawings and photographs

Unless otherwise stated photographs are by the author or Gordon Furness

Cover: Route of Keswick to Penrith turnpike at Lisco, Troutbeck. *Page 2:* The author at work. *Page 3,Top:* Map of route of Roman Road. B.P.Hindle. Roads & Tracks of the Lake District. Moorland Publishing Company. 1984. *Bottom:* Roman Milestone on A66 near Temple Sowerby. *Page 4. Top:* Sketch of Pack Horses. *Bottom:* Cartoon of Snuff Taker. Samuel Gawith web site. *Page 5.* Snuff Box in collection of Penrith Museum. Sydney Chapman. *Page 6. Top:* Map of Turnpikes in Cumbria J W Dunderdale, Kendal Brown. *Bottom:* Typical turnpike, sketch from The Milestone Society archives *Page 7:* Restored milestone on unclassified road at Wallthwaite. *Page 8:* Old Dungeon Ghyll Hotel circ 1806. Celebration of the Lake District, National Trust. *Page 9:* Kings Arms Hotel circ 1823 painting in the collection of Kendal Town Council *Page 12, Top:* Steam driven carriage. Ron Freethy.Turnpikes & Toll Houses of Lancashire. 1986. *Bottom:* Painting of Mrs Hutchinson. P. G. Hamerton . 1852. Owned by Mr & Mrs Bennett *Page 13:* Section of map. James Clarke. Survey of the Lakes. 1787. Cumbria County Library archives. *Page 14.* Cockell House, Drovers Road, Penrith. *Page 15:* Penrith Station circ 1906. Penrith, A Historical Record in Photographs, Eden District Council *Page 16 & 17:* Map showing route of 1762 Keswick to Penrith turnpike, Gordon Furness *Page 18, Top:* Royal Mail at Grasmere. Old Lakeland Transport. Irvine Hunt.Rusland Press. 1978. *Bottom:* LNWR 'Cauliflower' 'F 0-6-0 No.588409 approaching Troutbeck from Threlkeld. British Railways - Past & Present No.1 Cumbria. John Broughton & Nigel Harris. Silver Link Publishing. *Page 20:* Brigham Toll Bar Cottage, Keswick *Page 21:* ScalesToll Bar Cottage, Threlkeld *Page 22. Right:* Milestone on the A6 between Shap and Kendal *Left:* Damaged milestone near Allonby *Page 23, Right:* Syd Smith, Westcoe, surveying milestone at Shundraw Junction *Left:* Remnants of milestone at Far Howe *Page 24, Top left:.* Original plaque found on a house at Threlkeld *Top right:* Milestone at Woodend, Threlkeld during restoration *Bottom left:* Mark Robinson, stone mason, Lakeland Slate Products Limited, Keswick *Bottom right:* Stone prior to splitting and dressing. *Page 25 Top right:* Finished new milestones *Top left:* Preparing mould at Hexham Foundry, David Gosling *Centre right:* Casting plaques at Hexham Foundry, David Gosling *Bottom left:* Wilson's Haulage and Plant Limited installing milestone at Storms Farm *Page 27:* Part of an original Penrith and Keswick Turnpike Trust tender poster. Cumbria County Record Office, Carlisle. *Page 30,* Bottom: Toll Bar Cottage, Eamont Bridge circ 1904, Frank Boyd, Around Penrith, Budding Books *Page 31:* 1834 Annual Accounts for the Keswick Turnpike Trust. Cumbria County Records Office.